YOU & YOUR AMAZING BRAIN

Clive Gifford
Illustrated by Anne Wilson

words & pictures

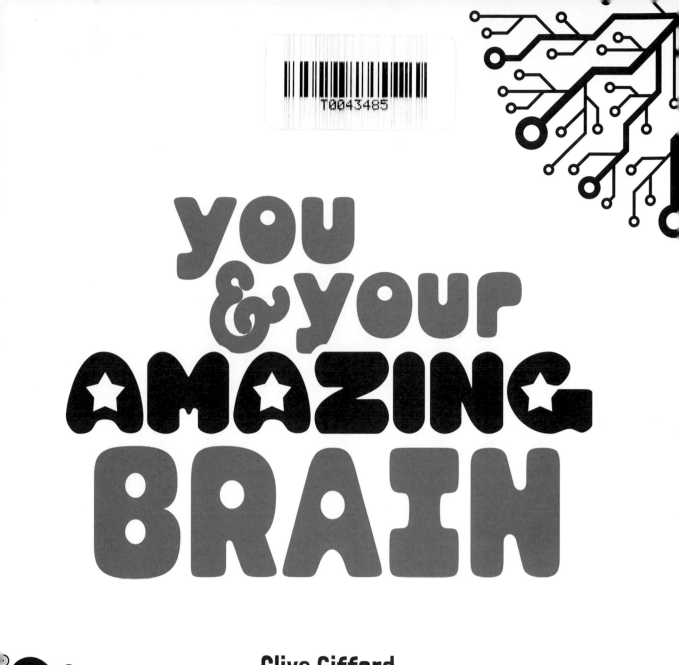

Brimming with creative inspiration, how-to projects, and useful information to enrich your everyday life, quarto.com is a favorite destination for those pursuing their interests and passions.

Designer: Karen Hood
Editor: Emily Pither
Assistant Editor: Alice Hobbs
Editorial Director: Rhiannon Findlay
Art Director: Susi Martin
Creative Director: Malena Stojic
Associate Publisher: Holly Willsher

This edition published
in 2023 by words & pictures,
an imprint of The Quarto Group.
100 Cummings Center, Suite 265D
Beverly, MA 01915, USA.
T (978) 282-9590 F (978) 283-2742
www.quarto.com

A CIP record for this book is available from the Library of Congress.

ISBN 978-0-7112-8362-6

Manufactured in Guangdong, China TT012023

987654321

CONTENTS

INTRODUCTION

If you're reading these words...well done! You are the proud owner of one of the greatest, most complex examples of engineering in nature—a human brain.

SMALL AND MIGHTY

The brain is more powerful than a room full of the latest computers, yet it uses less energy than a typical light bulb. It doesn't come with an instruction manual, but the more someone uses their brain, the better it works.

ANCIENT THINKING

Some ancient Chinese doctors thought that the brain was part of the kidneys, while the ancient Greek scientist Aristotle believed it kept the heart and blood cool. When the ancient Egyptians preserved a dead body to make a mummy, they thought so little of the brain that they used a hook to pull it out of the head through the nostrils, then threw it away.

ENDLESS POSSIBILITIES

The brain isn't much to look at—just a pinky-gray, jelly-like blob. But without it, we cannot survive. With it, we can achieve wonders: we can perform hundreds of different tasks; remember thousands of different facts, faces, and objects; invent new things and create new music, art, or stories never thought of before.

ALWAYS LEARNING

The brain can do SO many incredible things: it helps us understand the difference between right and wrong, learn and use more than one language, and imagine the future.

Recent advances in neuroscience—the study of the brain and nervous system—have revealed lots of surprising ways the incredible brain works. Not all brains work the same way, and this is something to be aware of and also celebrate.

One person may process or understand something one way, but that doesn't mean other people are going to see it in the same way.

Did you know that your brain constantly edits and alters your memories?

"Neurodiversity" describes the variation in brain function and social behaviors between different people. It's time to get our heads in the game and find out everything about brains, which all function a bit differently, but just as amazingly.

SECTION 1:

THE NAKED BRAIN

When it comes to thinking, problem-solving, and working through emotions, the brain is there to help. It's soft, squishy, and made up of different parts that often work together to keep people going all day and night.

At the center of the brain are parts that are similar to those found in other animals—known as the "primitive brain." What makes the human brain special is a large part called the cerebrum. It's this that gives humans their phenomenal processing power—greater than any supercomputer yet built.

All that power would go to waste if the brain couldn't communicate. Fortunately, it is hooked up to the rest of the body via an incredible network of nerves, senses, and chemical couriers, so that it can send and receive information from every part of the body...and from outside the body as well.

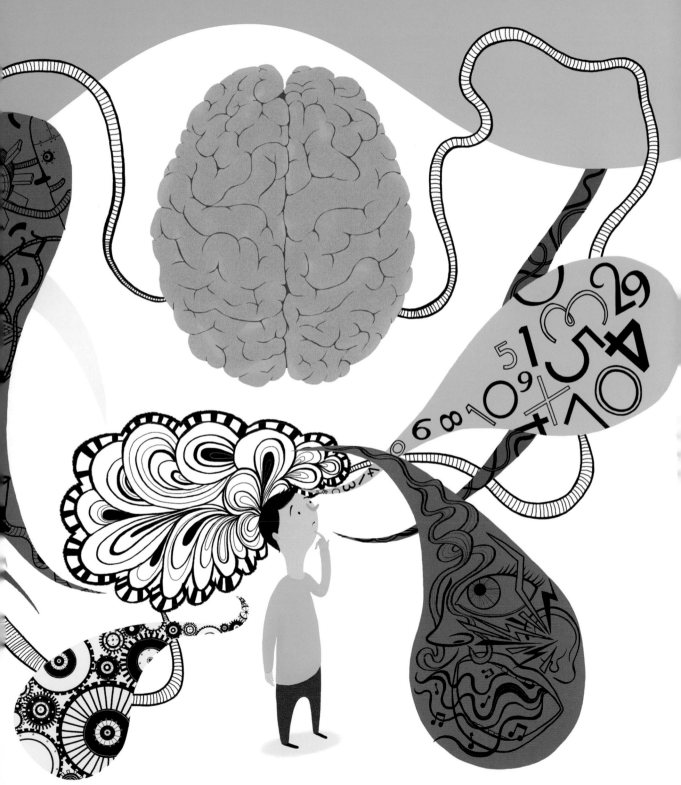

BRAIN IN A BOX

The precious human brain is about the size of a small cauliflower. It is delicate, but very well protected.

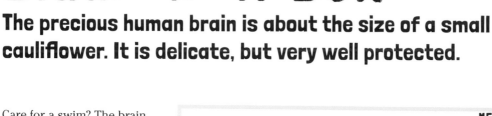

Care for a swim? The brain is buoyant, floating in up to 5 ounces of liquid that acts like a cushioning shock absorber. This fluid also offers protection by stopping the weight of the brain from pushing down on itself and the brain stem. The outer surface of the brain is wrapped up in sheets of thin but tough tissue called meninges. This all sits inside the bony crash helmet, the skull, which is made up of eight plates.

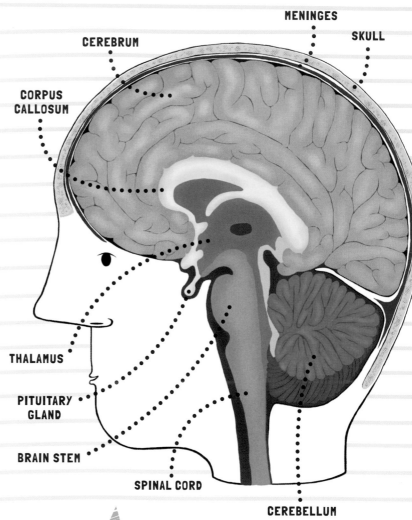

MENINGES

SKULL

CEREBRUM

CORPUS CALLOSUM

THALAMUS

PITUITARY GLAND

BRAIN STEM

SPINAL CORD

CEREBELLUM

ALMOST THREE-QUARTERS (73%) OF THE BRAIN IS MADE UP OF WATER.

The CEREBELLUM keeps us balanced and upright. It also controls small movements of the muscles.

The **BRAIN STEM** is responsible for keeping us ticking. It controls basic body functions, including breathing and the heartbeat.

WEIGHTY MATTERS

An adult human brain weighs 2.75 to 3 pounds, but it's not the biggest in the animal kingdom. A sperm whale's brain can weigh a mighty 17 pounds. In contrast, the mouse lemur has a teeny brain, the smallest of any mammal, weighing just 0.07 ounces.

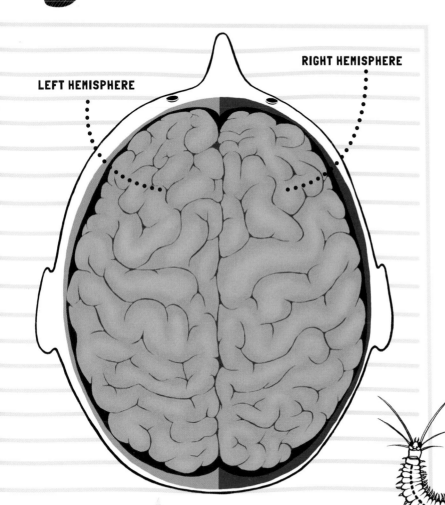

LEFT HEMISPHERE

RIGHT HEMISPHERE

The brain is formed in two halves, known as hemispheres. They're joined by a thick bundle of nerves called the corpus callosum. Think of this as a superfast broadband connection, made up of 200–250 million nerve fibers. This allows millions and millions of instructions and signals to flow between the two hemispheres every day. The brain is hooked up to the rest of the body by the brain stem, which connects it to the central nervous system that runs down through the spine.

The
CEREBRUM
is the biggest part of the brain and is where most of our thinking and problem-solving takes place.

MICROSCOPIC MIND
The *Platynereis dumerilii* ragworm has the smallest brain ever examined. It's only as big as the width of a human hair.

THE MAIN PARTS

The brain is made up of different parts, with the cerebrum being four-fifths of its entire weight. Scientists divide the cerebrum into four major parts called lobes. Each lobe performs different tasks.

FRONTAL LOBE
This is the control panel. Not only do we think, plan, learn, and solve problems using this lobe, it also processes complex emotions and helps create our personalities.

The cerebrum's outer surface, the cerebral cortex, is really wrinkly. The wrinkles increase the brain's surface area and its processing power. The head would have to be bigger than a beach ball if the cerebral cortex had all its wrinkles ironed out.

WHEN IRONED FLAT, THE CORTEX WOULD STRETCH OUT TO 16 FT^2.

TEMPORAL LOBE
This helps form memories and handles a person's sense of hearing, interpreting sounds and spoken language. In some people who are born deaf, the lobe adapts and helps interpret sign language.

PARIETAL LOBE

This lobe handles the senses of touch, temperature, and pain, as well as analyzing all the precise positions of the body's joints and muscles.

OCCIPITAL LOBE

The constant stream of information gathered by ably sighted people's eyes is processed mostly here. The lobe spots colors and movement, tries to identify objects, and judges distances. In blind people, the lobe's neurons rewire themselves to aid a person's other senses, including touch and hearing.

ROD OF IRON

In 1848, a yard-long iron rod blasted right through the skull of US railway worker Phineas Gage. Miraculously, he survived, but others noticed a drastic change in his personality. The accident destroyed some of his frontal lobe, and he experienced powerful emotions, which he expressed dramatically, and found it difficult to make decisions. It was the first time that neurologists began thinking about the different parts of the brain having different functions.

NERVE SUPERHIGHWAY

Every second, millions of tiny pulses of electricity whiz around the body, some faster than the quickest racing cars. These nerve impulses travel around the nervous system, mostly to and from the brain.

NERVES AND NEURONS

Humans are packed with up to 40 miles of nerves, each created from bundles of fibers that are made up of cells called neurons. Nerves extend through every part of the body. Motor nerves carry signals and commands from the brain to body parts, while sensory nerves carry signals from the body to the brain.

LEAP THE GAP

A neuron ends in tiny tendrils called dendrites at one end and branches called axons at the other. Each dendrite reaches out to neighboring neurons, forming microscopic gaps called synapses. For neurons to make connections, their nerve impulses have to cross the synapse using chemicals called neurotransmitters. This triggers an electrical impulse in the next neuron. Despite this complex journey, some nerve signals travel through the body at more than 250 mph.

The
CENTRAL NERVOUS SYSTEM
consists of the spinal cord and brain. It's a power-packed information superhighway.

NEURON NUCLEUS

DENDRITES

THE BRAIN RECEIVES 11 MILLION PIECES OF INFORMATION

BRAIN LAB

DIZZY DIRECTIONS

If a person lifts their right foot off the floor and rotates it clockwise at a regular pace, then draws repeated number sixes in the air with their index finger, starting at the top of the number, after a few sixes, the foot will have changed direction without the person noticing. Drawing number sixes involves a counterclockwise movement, so the brain switches the foot's direction to match.

LEFT AND RIGHT

The brain and nervous system are wired so that the left side of the brain controls the right side of the body and vice versa. Sometimes, one side of the brain gets a bit befuddled when trying to control two opposing movements on the same side in different directions.

AXON ENDS IN FINGERS CALLED TERMINALS

IMPULSE TRAVELS ALONG NEXT NEURON

ELECTRICAL IMPULSE IS AROUND ONE-TENTH OF A VOLT

FROM THE NERVOUS SYSTEM EVERY SECOND

RAPID RESPONSE

Some nerve actions bypass the brain and only travel to and from the spinal cord, which sends back a rapid response called a reflex. Reflexes protect us, and include coughing, sneezing, and withdrawing the hand when touching something hot or sharp.

MIND MESSENGERS

Nerves are not enough. We're also equipped with an incredible system of chemical messengers, called hormones, which influence when we eat, sleep, and how we grow. This is called the endocrine system.

INSTANT MESSENGERS

Hormones are created by organs such as the pancreas and stomach, or by small glands such as the thyroid and adrenal glands. Some, such as the growth hormone, act on the whole body. Others have specific purposes. For example, thyroxin helps control the speed at which the body's cells convert food into energy, known as the metabolic rate.

CHAIN OF COMMAND

For many glands, there is a chain of command, starting with a part of the brain called the hypothalamus. It checks that the body is well balanced and working okay, and if it isn't, sends signals to the pea-sized pituitary gland. This acts as a supervisor, sending hormones to command other glands and organs to release their hormones into the blood.

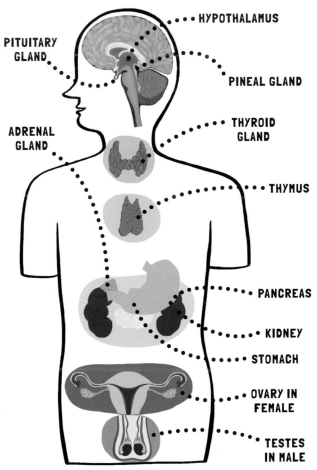

HYPOTHALAMUS

PITUITARY GLAND

PINEAL GLAND

THYROID GLAND

ADRENAL GLAND

THYMUS

PANCREAS

KIDNEY

STOMACH

OVARY IN FEMALE

TESTES IN MALE

CUDDLING CAN CAUSE SOME PEOPLE'S BODIES TO RELEASE OXYTOCIN, WHICH IS SOMETIMES CALLED A "HAPPY HORMONE" BECAUSE IT PROMOTES BONDING AND RELIEVES STRESS.

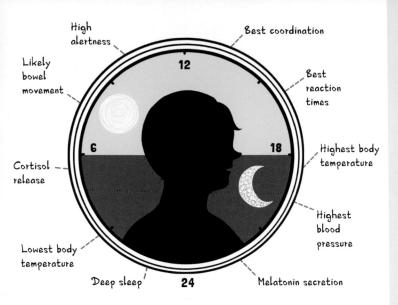

High alertness

Best coordination

Likely bowel movement

Best reaction times

12

6   18

Cortisol release

Highest body temperature

Highest blood pressure

Lowest body temperature

Deep sleep   24   Melatonin secretion

YOUR BODY CLOCK

Melatonin is a hormone released by the pineal gland when instructed by two clusters of brain cells in the hypothalamus. They're called the suprachiasmatic nuclei or SCN for short. The SCN acts as an internal timekeeper, using hormones. It plans a 24-hour cycle of activity, from body temperature changes to bowel movements. The SCN increases melatonin levels in the body during the evening to make us feel sleepy and reduces melatonin in the morning to make us feel alert.

CLOCK OFF

The SCN resets itself using light entering the eyes as a trigger. But when traveling long distances into other time zones, the body clock can get out of sync, leading to fatigue known as "jet lag."

TEEN TIME

Body clocks operate on slightly different timescales, making some people early starters and others night owls. Many teenagers' body clocks are set late, meaning they struggle to get to sleep or rise early.

8 FT, 3 IN

TOO MUCH GROWTH HORMONE MADE KURDISH MAN SULTAN KÖSEN GROW TO 8 FT, 3 IN TALL, BECOMING THE WORLD'S TALLEST MAN.

0

MAKING SENSE

The senses gather data about our surroundings and send it to the brain. They don't judge or measure the information they collect—that's a job for the brain.

BRAIN LAB

TRICK YOUR THERMOCEPTION

If someone were to chill two coins in a freezer for 20 minutes, then lay them on a table with a room-temperature coin, they could trick their thermoception into thinking all three were cold. First, they would need to touch the two cold coins with their forefinger and index finger and then touch the warmer coin with the middle finger—it would feel just as cold as the others.

MIND MYTH: WE HAVE FIVE SENSES

We know about taste, touch, sight, hearing, and smell, but neuroscientists think there are over a dozen senses! These include balance (equilibrioception), pain (nociception) and thermoception—being able to sense hot and cold.

EQUILIBRIOCEPTION

NOCICEPTION

THERMOCEPTION

WHERE'S MY ARM?

Proprioception is the sense of where a person's body parts are at any one time. By calculating joint angles and muscle movements needed, the brain tells the body how to do things like lifting arms above the head—even when the person's eyes are closed! Many people's brains keep on sending back data and sensations about an arm or leg even after it has been amputated (removed)—a phenomenon called phantom limb.

BRAIN LAB

FALL THROUGH THE FLOOR

Trick a friend's sense of proprioception by getting them to lie down, close their eyes, and relax. Lift their legs so they point straight upward and hold them up for two minutes. Then, lower the legs really slowly back to the floor. Many people report the alarming feeling of their legs falling through the floor, as their brain has forgotten their position and thinks they're already on the floor before they lower them!

EAR, EAR

A person's ears can gather sound waves, which travel as tiny vibrations. After they vibrate the eardrum, they are converted into electrical signals by the cochlea, before being sent along auditory nerves to the brain.

OSSICLES
are the three smallest bones in the body. They amplify vibrations from the sound waves

COCHLEA

EARDRUM

SOUND WAVES

SWITCHING OFF

Most people's ears never switch off, and they work even when people are asleep; it's just that the brain pays them next-to-no attention. Many brains are also skilled at filtering out background sounds, such as machinery or wind, when a person is awake, so they can concentrate on new or interesting sounds. Some people's brains don't filter in this way, and they may struggle to distinguish between sound types.

17

TASTE, TOUCH, AND SMELL

The senses are crucial to our survival, and they work differently in each of us.

SEEING SOUNDS, HEARING COLORS

Synesthesia is a rare condition where a person experiences one sense through another sense. For instance, when they hear certain sounds they might experience particular tastes.

A **HOMUNCULUS** is a figure whose parts are shown in proportion to how sensitive they are to touch.

TOUCHY FEELY

Just below the skin are millions of different touch receptor cells. They can distinguish vibrations, texture, and the difference between light and heavy pressure. They're not found evenly all over the body. The middle of the back, for example, has very few, while the lips and fingertips are jam-packed—making them extremely sensitive.

AS PEOPLE GROW OLDER, THEIR SENSE OF TASTE CAN WEAKEN OR CHANGE...

SNIFFING IT OUT

People can sense thousands, possibly millions, of different smells via two small patches of cells high up in the nose. The brain seeks out new smells but can get bored of familiar odors. Smells often conjure up memories from the past, when the olfactory bulb sends smell signals to the brain. This is closely linked with two parts of the brain responsible for creating memories—the amygdala and the hippocampus.

TASTY STUFF

The sense of taste relies on clumps of cells called taste buds found on the tongue, cheeks, and the roof of the mouth. They detect combinations of five different tastes: sweet, sour, salty, bitter, and umami (a savory taste found in mushrooms and meat). Taste relies heavily on smell. If someone held their nose and someone else fed them equal-sized chunks of apple and raw potato, it would be hard to tell the difference.

BRAIN LAB

TWO NOSES

A person's sense of touch can be confused by the Aristotle illusion. If someone crossed the middle and index fingers and used the V shape they created to touch their nose it would feel like they were touching two noses. This is because the brain deduces that the only way the outside of the two fingers can be both touching an object is that there are two of them—in this case, two noses.

OLFACTORY BULB

SMELL RECEPTOR CELLS

NASAL CHAMBER

TASTE BUDS

THIS IS WHY SOME ADULTS LIKE FOODS THEY HATED AS CHILDREN.

OUT OF SIGHT

Two small balls of jelly tell us more about the world than any other part of the body, especially when they're hooked up to the mighty brain. Welcome to the visual world.

LIGHT'S JOURNEY

Light enters the eye through the protective, clear cornea and then travels through the pupil, before it's focused by the lens to reach the back of the eyeball, called the retina. This is covered in over 100 million light-sensitive cells (cones to detect color and rods to detect light and dark) that convert light into electrical signals. These signals travel along the optic nerve to the brain, which figures out what we're actually seeing.

CILIARY MUSCLES
bend the lens to let a person focus on near or distant objects

Light is bent in the eye so that scenes are detected upside-down on the retina. The brain turns the image the right way up.

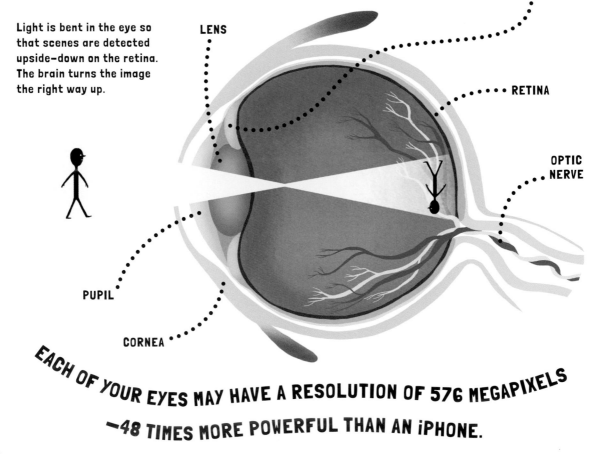

LENS

RETINA

OPTIC NERVE

PUPIL

CORNEA

EACH OF YOUR EYES MAY HAVE A RESOLUTION OF 576 MEGAPIXELS —48 TIMES MORE POWERFUL THAN AN iPHONE.

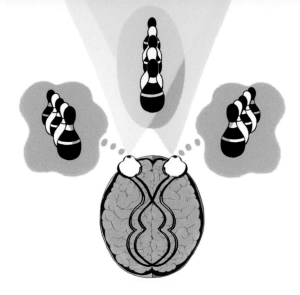

EYEBALL TO EYEBALL

Having two eyes mounted in the front of a person's head gives them the ability to perceive depth and see the world in three dimensions. Both eyes send back images of the same scene, and the brain calculates, from the slight difference in their views, the depth and distances from objects.

BRAIN LAB

HOLE IN THE HAND

See how the brain can sometimes merge views from both eyes in startling fashion. If a person was to look through a cardboard tube with their left eye while keeping their right eye open, and then move the palm of their right hand two-thirds of the way along the tube facing the right eye, after a short time they would see a hole appear in their hand. Yikes!

NOT PERFECT

Optical illusions either trick the physical workings of a person's actual eyes or mess with the brain and how it tries to make sense of the information the eyes send it. These are called perceptual illusions.

Stare at the two inner squares. Which one is lightest? The answer is that they're both the same color. Your brain sometimes perceives an object's color by how it compares to its surroundings. Here, it has been tricked by the darker and lighter borders into believing the central squares are different shades.

SMART SAFARI

How do other creatures' brains compare to ours? Well, some living things don't even try. Jellyfish, clams, and starfish don't have brains and rely, instead, on a network of nerves. Other creatures do have brains, but they are very different from our own.

GIANT SQUID

SEA SQUIRT

FOOD FOR THOUGHT

As sea squirts grow older, they settle in one place and no longer need their brain, so they digest it and its nutrients! In contrast, axolotls value their brains so highly that they can actually regrow parts of them if needed.

DANGEROUS DONUT

Despite measuring 43 feet long and tipping the scales at 1,100–1,520 pounds, the giant squid has a brain weighing the same as a lemon (3.5 ounces). What's more, it's shaped like a donut and its food runs right through a hole in its middle. The food is carried inside a half-inch-wide stretchy tube, so the squid cannot eat large chunks of food for fear of damaging its brain!

GIANT SQUID BRAIN

AXOLOTL

22

SLEEPING WHALE

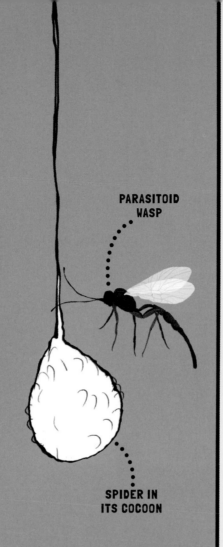

PARASITOID WASP

SPIDER IN ITS COCOON

MIGHTY MOUSE

A mouse's brain weighs less than 0.02 ounces yet may contain over 60 billion connections between its brain cells. This makes it more powerful than the fastest supercomputer yet built.

010001110011001011
001011000111001000
100010100100100100
111101110111000010100
101010110001010010100

MIND CONTROL

Some sneaky creatures have the ability to take over the brains of other species. The parasitoid wasp, for example, injects its eggs and a cocktail of chemicals inside a spider's body. The chemicals take control, instructing the spider to spin a cocoon around itself, rather than a web. The baby wasps develop inside this little sack, feeding on the defenseless spider when they hatch.

HALF ASLEEP

Some creatures, such as dolphins and whales, are able to half sleep. One half of their brain rests, while the other half remains alert and takes in information from the one eye that stays open. Yes, they sleep with one eye open!

SECTION 2:
MIND MECHANICS

The brain starts out smaller than one of the periods on this page. While in the womb, it grows fast. Throughout pregnancy, the fetus's brain builds up large numbers of brain cells called neurons. By the time a baby is born, they have almost 100 billion neurons inside their head.

It's not all over once a baby is born, though. The brain changes constantly throughout our lives. It takes in information from the senses and makes thousands of conscious decisions every day. It also stores vast numbers of facts and experiences as memories, by making and breaking connections between brain cells.

All this hard work takes a lot of resources. The busy brain requires a surprisingly large fraction of all the energy the body makes. It also requires water and sleep to function at its very best.

AN EVOLVING SCIENCE

Brains were poorly understood in the past, leading to harmful medical mistakes. Neuroscience is now trying to get to grips with how the brain really works, and we are still learning!

Am I BORING you?

HOLE IN THE HEAD

People were performing operations on one another's heads as far back as 6,000 years ago. One belief held that the head contained "evil spirits" that caused things like headaches or seizures, so surgeons would drill holes in the skull to let the spirits out. Ouch! Concerningly, this remained a popular way of dealing with many ailments until as recently as the 19th century.

SPIN ME AROUND

Spinning a patient around very quickly while strapped in a chair was once thought to reduce "brain congestion," which was a term used to describe a variety of conditions. This rotational therapy was pioneered by Erasmus Darwin (grandfather of the famous naturalist Charles Darwin), and practiced by US doctor Benjamin Rush. Perhaps unsurprisingly, it did little to help, and just made people feel dizzy and nauseous.

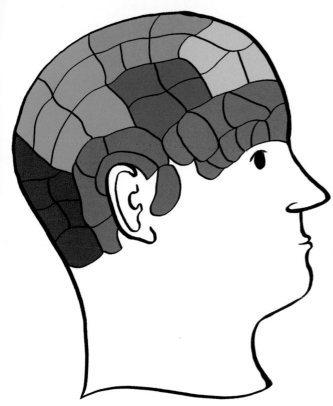

SCAN-TASTIC

From the 1970s onward, brain-scanning machines allowed scientists to explore and study working brains without performing surgery. Functional MRI (fMRI) scanners, for instance, show which brain areas are busy at a particular time by measuring the amount of oxygen carried in blood to certain brain parts. This has helped scientists learn how the brain performs particular tasks.

THE BRAIN FEELS NO PAIN, SO BRAIN SURGEONS CAN OPERATE WITH THE PATIENT AWAKE!

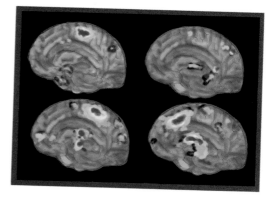

NO CHARGE

In 1964, Spanish doctor José Delgado inserted a transmitter into the brain of a radio-controlled charging bull. As the bull charged straight at Delgado, his radio transmitter sent signals to electrodes implanted in the bull's brain. These electrodes instructed the bull's muscles to move, stopping it from charging.

NEURODIVERSITY

Recent advances in science have taught us that brains are more varied and wonderful than we thought before. Scientists have discovered new types of brain cell and are learning how people with neurodiverse brains (which function a little differently than others) are natural variations of the human brain, just like differing hair colors. Neurodiverse brains have their own strengths and weaknesses.

BRAINY BUILDING BLOCKS

Let's delve deep inside the brain and look at the cells that make it so special. These cells are responsible for everything we do, and there are billions of them!

A single neuron can send 1,000 electrical signals each second.

NEURONS

Remember neurons, those busy little cells we looked at on pages 12 and 13? Well, they make up around half the bulk of the brain—and there are 86 billion of them in total! These are the cells responsible for thinking, acting, learning, and making memories. Neurons communicate with each other using electrical signals and neurotransmitter chemicals. Each neuron can have more than 10,000 links to other neurons, forming complicated webs known as neural networks.

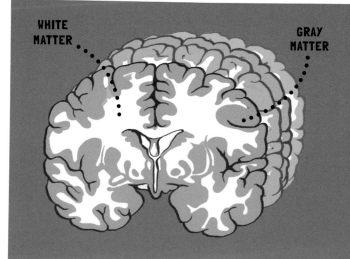

WHITE MATTER

GRAY MATTER

GRAY AND WHITE

The top fraction of an inch of the brain—the cerebral cortex—is packed full of the nuclei of neurons. This is the gray matter. Beneath it lies white matter, which is mostly full of axons (the long tails of neurons). The proportions of gray and white matter in the brain change at different times in our lives.

IT'S NOT ALL NEURONS

Even though they are barely talked about, other brain cells exist—and are pretty important! It's thought there are around 100 billion glial cells, which come in different types, including star-shaped cells called astrocytes. These act as a frame, holding neurons in place and supplying the nutrients that neurons need to perform.

ASTROCYTE

MICROGLIA

Microglia are the brain's security task force. These glial cells make up to about a tenth of all the cells in the brain. They detect unhealthy and damaged neurons, and may attack and digest unwanted brain intruders such as bacteria or viruses.

PLASTIC FANTASTIC

The brain's neurons have the remarkable ability to change connections throughout a person's life. This ability, called neuroplasticity, allows people to learn and store memories, among other things. Whenever a new skill or memory is formed, a large number of neurons create connections. These are strengthened each time they're active, which is why revising facts or practicing a new skill helps to reinforce it in the brain.

BOUNCING BACK

Plasticity can enable people to overcome brain injuries. Sometimes, neurons in other parts of the brain are able to link up to perform the tasks previously carried out by the damaged brain area.

DETOUR

MY, HOW YOU'VE GROWN!

The brain starts out as a tiny tube of cells too small for the human eye to see. It develops and changes both before and after a child is born.

BRAIN AT BIRTH

Those nine months or so in the womb see some serious brain building. New neurons are produced at rates of 250,000 every minute. Despite this feverish rate, the brain we're born with is still very much a work in progress. It may contain almost all the neurons; it's just that all the connections between them are yet to develop.

FAST GROWER

A newborn baby's brain weighs around a pound but packs on the weight fast. In the first 90 days of life, it grows around 1% a day as it starts making more and more connections (synapses) between its neurons. At the same time, the baby becomes more aware of the world around it. All this building work comes at a cost—up to 60% of a 0–3-month-old baby's energy is used for brain building!

We start to become aware of ourselves from 18 months onward, recognizing that the face in the mirror is ours!

BRAIN GROWTH

Four weeks after conception, the part of the fetus that will become the brain is smaller than a period on this page. The brain develops rapidly in the womb and continues to grow after a baby is born.

16 WEEKS

2.5 IN³
the same volume as a golf ball

22 WEEKS

6 IN³
about two small chicken eggs

HAPPY BIRTHDAY, BRAIN!

The brain on a child's sixth birthday is about four times bigger in volume than when they were born. It's now 90–95% of its adult size, but there are lots more changes in store. The number of synapses between neurons increases rapidly—a young child may have twice as many synapses as an adult. Some individual neurons may have more than 15,000 links to other neurons.

FASTER WITH FAT

A fatty substance called myelin covers the axons of neurons, a little like plastic insulation around electric wiring. The myelin helps signals travel much faster, giving the brain a major upgrade in processing power. Only the busiest neurons get the boost, which occurs at different points in life. A burst of myelination in the frontal lobe during the tween and teen years usually results in improved decision-making and planning skills.

LEARN, BABY, LEARN

The vast number of connections between neurons mean children can learn quickly and even easily. The brain prioritizes finding out new things but it is still figuring out how to focus its attention, which can be a little tricky when there's so much new stuff to learn.

30 WEEKS
15 IN³
about the same size as a satsuma

AT BIRTH
21 IN³
similar volume to a standard drink can

90 DAYS OLD
34 IN³
about the same size as a large orange

ADULT (MALE) BRAIN
78 IN³
about the size of two adult hands scrunched up into fists

THE TEENAGE BRAIN

The teenage years are a time of HUGE change in the body and mind. The brain undergoes a major makeover during the teen years and into the twenties.

MAKING CUTBACKS

Starting in late childhood and carrying on through the teen years, the brain makes major cutbacks. It cuts millions upon millions of connections between neurons that aren't used or which your brain thinks are no longer important. This process is called synaptic pruning because it's like pruning a tree. The weaker stems or branches are removed so that the remainder can grow stronger.

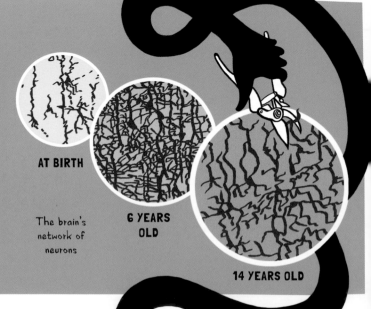

USE IT!

OR LOSE IT!

GETTING ORGANIZED

As a result, the brain's gray matter decreases but the connections that remain grow stronger. By the late teens or twenties, the pruned brain may be a little less flexible and finds it takes more effort to learn, but it can think about far more complex things and focus on a single problem for longer.

AT BIRTH

The brain's network of neurons

6 YEARS OLD

14 YEARS OLD

LONG FORGOTTEN

In the rush to streamline the brain, some things get lost, particularly personal memories from before the age of four or five—scientists call this childhood amnesia.

> What was my first teddy bear called?

BACK TO FRONT

Work on remodeling the brain begins at the back and gradually works forward. Last to get the full treatment are parts of the brain's frontal lobe, which are responsible for logical thinking, planning, and controlling thoughts and actions.

LEFT BEHIND

While lots of brain functions race ahead, some develop more slowly. One example is prospective memory—the ability to remember to do something in the future. It develops in childhood and into the twenties but not so much during the teen years. Others are proprioception and fine motor skills, which struggle to keep up with teenage growth spurts—and that's why some teens might find themselves walking into things or knocking things over more often than usual.

SUPER SOCIAL

The teenage brain can crave contact with others. It's the main way people build their beliefs about the world and learn how the world sees them. When thinking about social situations and comparing themselves to others, teens actually use more parts of their pre-frontal cortex than adults—proof that it's really important to them.

HIGH MAINTENANCE

The brain is great—it does so much—but it's also super demanding. Being on the go 24/7 requires tons of energy. The brain is one high-maintenance organ.

In some ways the brain is remarkably energy-efficient. All the mighty plans, creative thoughts, genius ideas, and learning, plus the day-to-day control of the body, sees the brain use the equivalent of just 12–24 watts of electrical power—enough to light a single low-energy bulb.

Yet, in other ways, it's a real power hog. The brain comprises only one-fiftieth of the body weight but uses around one-fifth of all of the energy and oxygen. Teenagers have a LOT going on—from growth spurts and puberty to all the new learning they're doing at school and in social situations. This means the brain makes huge demands on the body's energy supplies. This is why experts recommend a super-healthy, energy-packed diet for active teens. The body and brain need it!

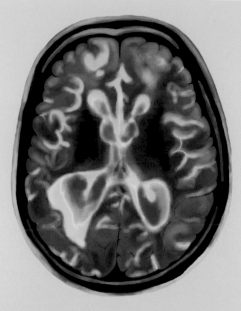

MIND MYTH:
WE ONLY USE 10% OF OUR BRAIN

This old myth has been disproven using brain-scanning machines. These show how all or almost all parts of a person's brain are active at different times of a typical day.

WATER WORKS

AMAZING FACT ALERT: The brain is 73% water. However, as we lose some H_2O during the course of the day, it's important that we replace it. Even a 1% drop in hydration can affect our ability to concentrate and store new things in our memory. A 2% or higher drop can lead to issues when problem-solving or decision-making. Keep your liquid levels topped up with regular drinks of water.

MIND GYM

Energy and oxygen reach the brain via 400 miles of blood vessels. Blood flows through these at a rate of 25–34 ounces of blood every minute, pumped relentlessly by the heart. Exercise improves blood flow and increases how much oxygen we take in, boosting brain performance. Recent studies have shown exercise even improves memory.

BRAIN LAB

LOW ENERGY = LOW PERFORMANCE?

Open a book index and read 20 entries. Then write down a random mobile phone number and add the digits up. Now try to write down all the index entries you can remember. Try this task at your liveliest, such as mid-morning, then when you're really tired, such as after a long day or just before bedtime. Do you notice a difference? Chances are you were able to remember more when you were the most awake.

THE GREAT MEMORY MACHINE

The brain is equipped with a phenomenal memory machine. It sifts through the millions of moments a person experiences and stores many they want to remember, as well as a few they'd prefer not to!

SENSORY MEMORY

Information from all of the senses enters the sensory memory for a fleeting moment. It might be the smell of a flower, a phrase shouted in the street, or words a person reads. If they don't pay any further attention to it, it is likely to leave sensory memory and be lost for good.

SHORT-TERM MEMORY

Any experience, fact, or other sensation in sensory memory that's of interest to the brain may be moved to the short-term memory. This has a surprisingly small capacity—it's thought only able to hold seven different things at one time and all for a maximum of 15–30 seconds, so as not to get cluttered. If the memory is not thought about again, chances are it will be thrown out and forgotten.

H.M.'S HIPPOCAMPUS

Scientists believe a pair of small seahorse-shaped parts of the brain called the hippocampus act like a gateway between short- and long-term memory. A patient known as H.M. had most of his hippocampus removed in the 1950s. While memories created before his surgery could still be recalled, H.M. could not form any new long-term memories.

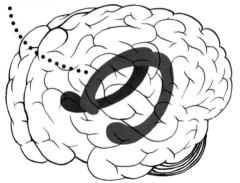

THE HIPPOCAMPUS

LONG-TERM MEMORY

If a person pays enough attention to something in their short-term memory, it may be filed away in the long-term memory. This is distributed all over the brain and has close-to-unlimited storage, so don't worry about maxing out the capacity. Each memory is stored as a collection of linked neurons. These neurons can potentially all fire together in the future to reproduce the memory. Long-term memories can last a lifetime.

BRAIN LAB

One way to increase the short-term memory performance is to break down information into small pieces. Try memorizing some 12-digit numbers as a whole and then by breaking them into chunks of three digits, i.e. 417 900 864 552. Many find chunked numbers easier to memorize and recall.

MIND MYTH: GOLDFISH HAVE THREE-SECOND MEMORIES

Goldfish are underestimated! Scientists in Israel trained goldfish to associate a certain sound with their feeding time. Five months later, the sound was replayed and the goldfish swam up, expecting food.

THANKS FOR THE MEMORIES

Can you remember what you had for dinner last Wednesday? How about the color of the last car you saw? If those details caught your interest, it's because they were encoded and stored in the long-term memory.

US AND THE WORLD

There are different types of long-term memories. Procedural memory recalls how to perform an action or skill, such as tying a knot or diving into a swimming pool. Semantic memory concerns knowledge, including facts and meanings. Episodic memories are all about us—from where we have been to what emotions we felt at certain moments.

"Last time I tried to dive, I belly-flopped and it hurt!"
—EPISODIC MEMORY

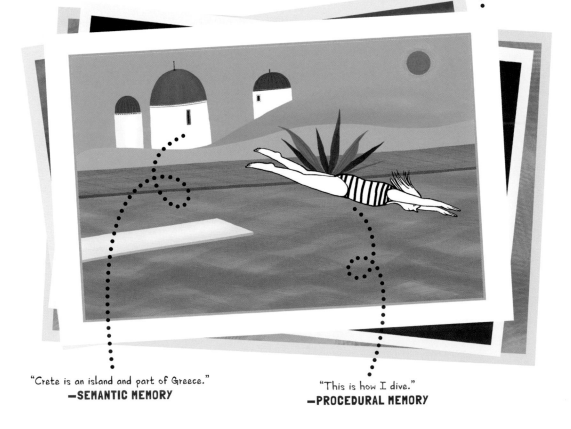

"Crete is an island and part of Greece."
—SEMANTIC MEMORY

"This is how I dive."
—PROCEDURAL MEMORY

MEMORY RECALL

When recalling a moment such as a great meal on vacation, the brain retrieves a large number of separate but related memories stored in different locations. These might include the food's look, taste, and smell, the people there for the meal, and what they said.

WELL REMEMBERED

Some memories are more easily retrieved than others due to their importance, because they conjure up strong emotions or because they're recalled frequently. Sometimes painful memories are the most easily remembered, because the high **stress** levels at the time of the event cause greater activity from the brain. The more connections between neurons a memory has, the easier and more likely it can be accessed later.

PTSD

Some people who have experienced extremely distressing events may find themselves reliving them. Intense memories can create nightmares and flashbacks where the person feels as if they are experiencing the traumatic event again. PTSD sufferers often experience anxiety and may have trouble sleeping and interacting with others.

SHIFTING MEMORIES

The brain sometimes edits and overwrites memories, inserting information from the present into the past. It's why many people remember an event long ago but can only recall the people present as they look now.

BRAIN LAB

TRAY TEST

See how many of these objects you can memorize. First, look at them for 30 seconds. Then, close this book, wait several minutes, and try to recall them all. If you get 15 or more, well done! Try this test again with 20 random words.

39

MEMORY MASTERS

Some people are memory masters. People like Nischal Narayanan from India who in 2006, at the age of 11, took only 12 minutes to memorize 225 random objects and then recalled them all correctly. Awesome!

MEMORY MAKEOVER

We're not all interested in competing in the World Memory Championships, but we can still improve our memory. A good night's sleep is a great start, as is giving a memory task full attention. We can help send something to our long-term memory through a process called rehearsal. This is where we repeat something we've learned, such as revising work or facts the next day, or practicing a skill again and again.

BRAIN LAB

HOW MANY CARDS?

Shuffle a deck of cards, and then try to memorize and recall the order of the first 10 cards—no peeking. If you succeed, try increasing the number of cards. At the World Memory Championships each year, some competitors can recall all the cards of seven complete, shuffled packs—364 cards in total!

CLARK'S NUTCRACKER BIRD BURIES 20,000 PINE SEEDS EACH YEAR

MAKING ASSOCIATIONS

Involving different parts of the brain in encoding a memory can lead to stronger connections, which is why some people write things down, read them out loud, or try to link things to pictures in their mind. Linking a new fact to something already familiar is called an association. People can associate pictures with words—a chef in a field for the city of Sheffield, for instance.

MEMORY AIDS

Mnemonics are simple memory aids where a person uses the first letter of each word they want to remember to make a phrase, such as Every Good Boy Does Fine for the order of the musical notes on a staff (E, G, B, D, F). Can you create a mnemonic for the planets and their order from the Sun: Mercury, Venus, Earth, Mars, Jupiter, Saturn, Uranus, Neptune? The stranger the sentence, the more memorable it may be to the brain.

My Very Eager Mother Just Served Us Nachos!

IN DIFFERENT PLACES, AND CAN REMEMBER WHERE THEY ALL ARE.

SLEEP ON IT

By the time someone is 70, they will have spent over 20 years asleep. Think of it as the brain's way of coping with being awake! Sleep is valuable and complex; more goes on while we snooze than people think.

STAGES OF SLEEP

A night's sleep consists of three stages of ever-deeper sleep and a lively stage known as rapid eye movement (REM). People cycle through these stages over a 90-minute period. REM sleep occurs after the brain stem sends out a burst of nerve signals. The heart and breathing rates increase, the eyes move rapidly behind the closed eyelids, and the brain is very active. This lasts just 5–15 minutes but during this period, people can dream vividly.

DREAMS

Everyone dreams, even if they cannot recall much after waking. Their purpose is unclear, but many experts think it's the brain's way of housekeeping and tidying up experiences, memories, and connections from the day before.

WHY SLEEP?

Sleep is vital for a number of reasons.

It gives both the body and brain time for rest and repair. The heart slows and nerve signals to many muscles are interrupted so they're not on the move, meaning people don't hurt themselves physically acting out their dreams.

The body produces new cerebrospinal fluid at night. This washes through the brain helping clean out any waste products that have built up and might harm it in the future.

Memories and newly learned skills are encoded and moved to more permanent places in long-term memory. They may also be linked with other, earlier memories to make them easier to retrieve in the future.

Connections between different collections of neurons are built and strengthened during sleep. This can sometimes lead to a person waking up with a miraculous solution to a problem they were fretting about the day before.

SLEEP CYCLE

STAGE 1:	STAGE 2:	STAGE 3:	STAGE 4:
LIGHTEST (1–7 mins) Heart and breathing slow. Muscles relax.	**LIGHT (10–25 mins)** Heart slows further. Eye movement stops.	**DEEP (20–40 mins)** Brain waves slow down. Most refreshing sleep.	**REM (20–40 mins)** Eyes move rapidly. Brain, heart, and breathing increase.

SECTION 3:

SO MUCH TO TAKE IN

Everybody's brain is slightly different, but each is a remarkable piece of natural engineering. It allows us to learn, feel, plan, think up new ideas, and communicate using language in a variety of ways —an extraordinary achievement for a 3-pound blob of tofu-like material crammed inside the skull.

Brilliant as it is, the brain remains far from perfect. It takes shortcuts when it can, makes assumptions that are sometimes plain wrong, and often just makes a guess to save time. The brain doesn't always see eye to eye with the rest of the body, sometimes ignores important information because it's overwhelmed by emotions, and can even make imagined events seem true and real.

The brain can also be influenced by how people see themselves and what they believe others think of them. It can be swayed into making decisions by people's fears, passions, and attitude to risk.

GUESSING GAMES AND THE BRAIN

Do you like guessing games? The brain does. The brain makes guesses all the time.

No wonder the brain makes guesses, the poor thing's bombarded with millions of pieces of information every day. To save time and energy, the brain makes its best guess, often based on what it has learned.

M1ND5 C4N DO 4M4Z1NG 7H1NG3

PATTERN RECOGNITION

The brain sometimes seeks out patterns it can recognize, which works remarkably well most of the time. For example, it's possible to read this message even though it's made of jumbled up letters.

But this method can sometimes lead the brain to spot familiar patterns when none truly exist, such as faces in clouds, food, or on everyday objects. This is called pareidolia, and neuroscientists think it occurs in the brain's temporal lobes, which contain lots of neurons desperate to spot faces—we are social animals, after all.

AOCCDRNIG TO RSCEEARH,

IT DEOSN'T MTTAER IN WAHT OREDR

TEH LTTEERS IN A WROD ARE,

THE OLNY IPRMOETNT TIHNG IS TAHT THE FRIST

AND LSAT LTTEER ARE IN TEH RGHIT PCLAE.

FUNNY FACES

We can have fun tricking our face recognition.
Does this picture look like a regular smiling
upside down face? Turn it around…you'll be
surprised! Why didn't you spot it before? Because
the brain guesses wrongly that all is in order after
it has spotted familiar facial features like eyes and
mouths the right way up.

FILLING IN THE GAPS

The brain also fills in gaps in knowledge,
images, and sounds with what it expects to
be there. This works well but isn't foolproof.

If the brain doesn't get the whole picture
from the eyes, it will use its best guess
to fill in the gaps. This technique can
sometimes be tricked with optical illusions.
They can make the brain believe a shape
is present when it really isn't.

There is no actual ball
with spikes sticking
out of it.

Do you see two triangles?
Of course you do! But they're
the work of your brain; all that
is really there are three
incomplete black circles and
three arrowheads.

These images only feature series of black
and white lines. The oval, rectangle, and
circle you think you see aren't actually
drawn on the images.

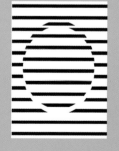

OVAL?   RECTANGLE?   CIRCLE?

MAKING ASSUMPTIONS

Part of the brain's guesswork is based on making assumptions. These are speedy but sometimes inaccurate shortcuts based on previous experience. They are used to make sense of images, sounds, and also facts. They're designed to speed everything UP but can sometimes slow understanding DOWN.

For instance, try to answer the following riddle.

Boxer A was Boxer B's son, but Boxer B was not Boxer A's father? How's that possible?

ANSWER: Because Boxer B was Boxer A's mother.

KEEPING IT IN PERSPECTIVE

The brain often makes assumptions about the information it receives from the senses when trying to make sense of a scene. This includes rules of perspective—how things stretch off into the distance and how light and shadows tend to work. These assumptions can be tricked by optical illusions. Give these brain games a try and see for yourself.

SEE THE SEESAW

Which side of the seesaw is sloping downward? Look more closely and grab a ruler. You'll be surprised. The seesaw is perfectly level, but the brain assumes the triangle on the right side is a weight pushing that side down.

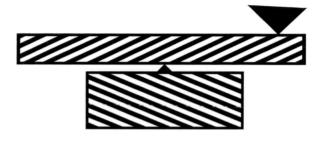

TWO TABLES

Which table is longer? Neither—they're the same size! Because of the perspective, the brain makes us think that the table on the left stretches off into the distance. Therefore, we assume that the table on the left is longer, because the vertical lines appear longer than the same-length horizontal lines that make up the table on the right.

SNEAKY CHESS

Check out this great puzzle from American scientist Edward H. Adelson. Which chessboard square is lighter, A or B? Surely, it's B, but you'll be stunned to learn they are both precisely the same shade! The brain assumes square B is a light square on a chessboard, just covered in shadow cast by the cylinder. So, we perceive the square as far lighter than square A.

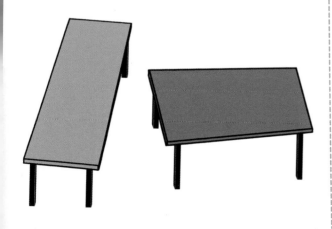

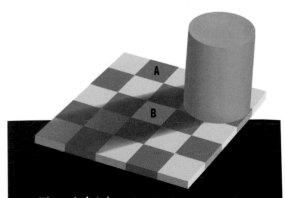

If you don't believe it, cut out some paper to mask out the rest of the picture except for the two squares. Awesome isn't it?

THINK ABOUT IT

We have thousands of thoughts every day, many of which we don't even know about. Some of this unconscious thinking can unfairly influence decisions and judgments because of systematic errors called cognitive biases.

Why, why, why?

What does it mean?

What shall I have for lunch?

ARE YOU SURE?

SKEWED THINKING / BRAIN BIASES

Cognitive biases can affect how you judge information, store memories, and make choices. Some may help speed up your brain's decision-making and be relatively harmless. Others can be extremely harmful and contribute to racism, sexism, and other damaging prejudices.

AFFINITY BIAS is the tendency to get along with others whom the brain thinks are like you and to agree with and adopt their views without fully examining them.

FAMILIARITY BIAS is where we feel calmer and more positive toward familiar things, so when shopping, for example, we are more likely to choose brands and objects we're familiar with— a reason why companies spend billions bombarding us with advertising!

AVAILABILITY BIAS sees us value information that springs to mind over harder-to-recall facts we may actually need to make a good decision. It's a bit like grabbing the first book at a library rather than searching the shelves for the best book on the subject.

I'm not an expert, but I think...

Is that true?

Why does that make me upset?

How do I get there?

NOT SEEING BOTH SIDES

People are more likely to believe something is true if it backs up what they already thought or suspected. This is called confirmation bias, and it can stop us from looking at both sides of a debate or getting all the information we need to make informed judgements.

NOT MY FAULT

The brain likes to take the credit when something goes right and blame others when something goes wrong. Classic examples are a poor driver blaming other motorists and someone complaining about their teacher, textbooks, or stuffy classroom when failing a test. Apart from being unfair to others, this bias blinds us to the ways we can improve—and stops us from learning and growing!

BRAIN LAB

THE HALO EFFECT

This bias sees us overvalue the words and deeds of someone we admire or find attractive. So, people may be more likely to believe a celebrity idol or social media influencer's opinion over a genuine expert on that topic.

FALSE MEMORY

Biases, flawed thinking, and memory errors can lead people to have memories of things that are wrong or didn't happen. We can create a simple false memory in someone else's mind using the power of suggestion. Write down a list of words associated with sleep, such as "bed," "pillow," "snooze," "snore," "nap," "rest," and "dream," but don't include the word "sleep" itself. Ask a few people to memorize your list, then ask them if they can remember the words a few hours later. When they recall the words, many will have a false memory of "sleep" being on the list.

MIND YOUR LANGUAGE

There's one power humans have that's quite unlike any other: the power of language. Visual, written, and spoken language forms the foundation of how we express everything from complex ideas to gossip and instructions.

THE SPOKEN WORD...SEEN AND HEARD!

Language is heard, understood, seen, and spoken using a number of different parts of the brain. Even a simple greeting involves significant brainpower.

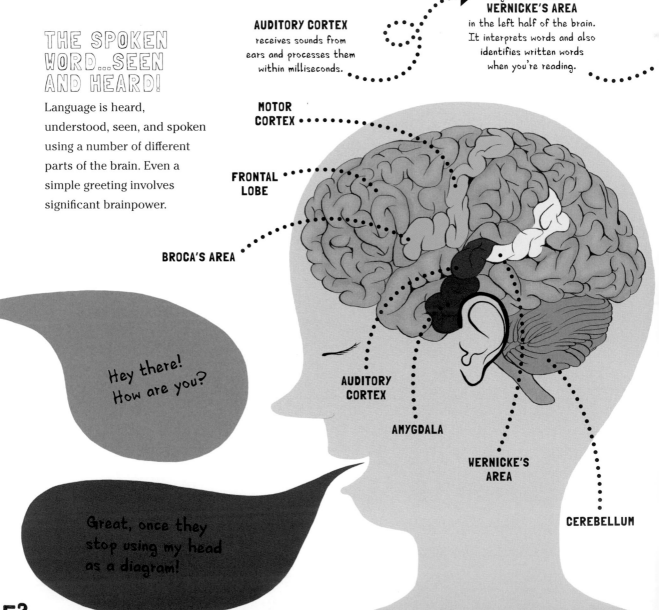

AUDITORY CORTEX receives sounds from ears and processes them within milliseconds.

Signals are sent to **WERNICKE'S AREA** in the left half of the brain. It interprets words and also identifies written words when you're reading.

MOTOR CORTEX

FRONTAL LOBE

BROCA'S AREA

AUDITORY CORTEX

AMYGDALA

WERNICKE'S AREA

CEREBELLUM

Hey there! How are you?

Great, once they stop using my head as a diagram!

THERE ARE OVER 6,900 DIFFERENT SPOKEN LANGUAGES AND OVER 300 SIGN LANGUAGES IN THE WORLD, MANY UTILIZED BY MILLIONS.

The **AMYGDALA** judges the emotional tone of the spoken words. Is the tone threatening or soothing, humorous or sarcastic?

Different memories may be accessed throughout the brain to fully understand the words spoken. The **FRONTAL LOBE** may figure out the full meaning of what has been said.

Once the brain has selected what words the person wants to say back, **BROCA'S AREA** picks the movements of your throat, mouth, and lips needed to voice the reply.

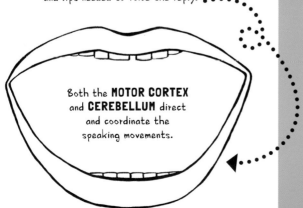

Both the **MOTOR CORTEX** and **CEREBELLUM** direct and coordinate the speaking movements.

NONVERBAL LANGUAGES

There are other ways to communicate besides speech. Facial expressions, gestures and poses (body language) can communicate a person's mood. Different sign languages involving hand gestures exist, such as Libras in Brazil and British Sign Language (BSL) in the UK. These enable instant communication between those unable to produce or hear speech—from hearing impaired people to divers working underwater.

STARTING YOUNG

Babies recognise many basic language sounds within six months. A two-year-old may know 300 words, and by secondary school age a child may know over 10,000! Child and teen brains are really good at picking up a second and even a third language. When Belgian Johan Vandewalle was in his teens he could hold conversations in 22 languages!

BRAIN LAB

ASL

American Sign Language (ASL) has a different hand signal for each letter of the alphabet. It also has single gestures for common words or phrases to save time. Look up the whole alphabet and then practise using it with your friends or family. See if you can memorise your favourite words or phrases and hold a conversation.

INTELLIGENCE

Every single human on this Earth is intelligent. One person's intelligence might not look exactly the same as another person's, and that's a great thing: we each have unique strengths and ways in which we work things out.

MORE THAN ONE

Many experts believe we have not one but lots of different forms of intelligence. Lucky us! These include linguistic intelligence (language skills) and musical intelligence— the ability to recognize and use rhythms, pitch, and notes. We all have different amounts of these. So, someone may be a genius with words but struggle a bit with math or not be so good at music.

ME AND YOU

Several forms of intelligence are about our ability to understand ourselves (intrapersonal intelligence) or how others tick (interpersonal intelligence). People with high levels of this latter intelligence are sociable, good at interacting with others, and can read others' nonverbal communication well. They can put themselves in other people's shoes to understand how they might be feeling.

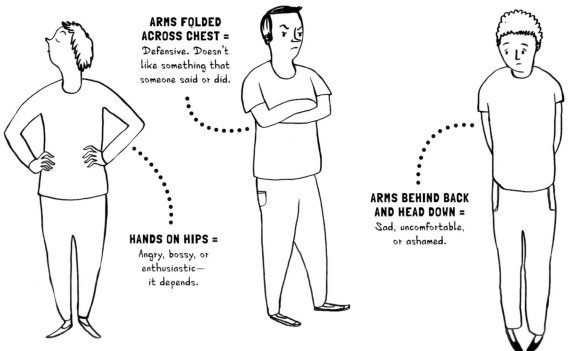

ARMS FOLDED ACROSS CHEST =
Defensive. Doesn't like something that someone said or did.

HANDS ON HIPS =
Angry, bossy, or enthusiastic— it depends.

ARMS BEHIND BACK AND HEAD DOWN =
Sad, uncomfortable, or ashamed.

HEAD FOR NUMBERS

Mathematical-logical intelligence is the ability to deal with sums, equations, and logical arguments. It enables people to spot patterns in data, crunch numbers, and analyze scientific and engineering problems. Challenge your own abilities by trying to build a sum equaling 1,000 from four addition signs and eight number 8s.

ANSWER: 888+88+8+8+8 = 1,000

WATCH THIS SPACE

Visual-spatial intelligence allows people to judge, understand, and manipulate shapes, spaccs, and images. We rely on this to spot small visual changes in people, placcs, and objects, as well as understanding maps, charts, and graphs, and judging speeds and distances when cycling or playing sports.

SMARTER TOGETHER

Neurodiverse people experience and interpret the world in their own way. These differences allow for unique forms of intelligence. Varied brain function can lead to exciting new ideas and creative ways to solve problems. We need brains of all varieties for true intelligence!

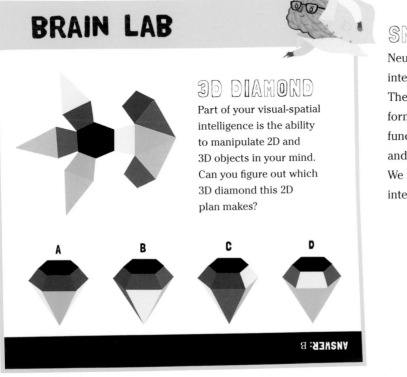

BRAIN LAB

3D DIAMOND

Part of your visual-spatial intelligence is the ability to manipulate 2D and 3D objects in your mind. Can you figure out which 3D diamond this 2D plan makes?

A   B   C   D

ANSWER: B

Ahhh!

PROBLEM-SOLVING

Problems can be tackled and solved in many ways. The brain weighs up the alternatives, makes calculations, and then selects the best solution... most of the time.

TRY, TRY AGAIN

The brain is wired to recognize patterns in a problem and may also spot connections with information already stored in the memory. Both can yield solutions to problems. Sometimes, people may need to employ trial and error, testing out possible solutions, and if they fail, feeding back any useful things they've learned to help inform their next attempt.

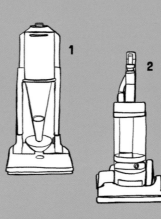

British inventor James Dyson built 5,127 prototypes of his bagless cyclonic vacuum cleaner before he found one that worked—that's some serious trial and error!

BRAIN LAB

LOGICAL LEMONS

Logical thinking takes known facts and uses them to draw new conclusions. The brain uses logic frequently to solve math equations and other problems. Here's an example. Carrie sold half her crate of lemons at the market, then gave away a quarter of those remaining. After losing four on the way home, she was left with 11. How many lemons did she start with?

ANSWER: 40

NO ONE SOLUTION

Occasionally, the brain gets in a fix and two solutions seem equally correct. This is the case with ambiguous images. These illusions are created so that the brain perceives two equally likely answers. Unable to settle on one, the brain flits between the two. Stare at the following images. Do you see a vase or two faces in the first and a bird or a rabbit in the second? <u>The answer in both cases is probably both!</u>

BRAINSTORMING BOOST

Brainstorming is thinking up as many ideas or solutions as possible without judging each idea… at first. Best performed with others, once everyone's out of ideas, you return to examine each idea in detail. Working together in this way can lead to a brilliant solution, sometimes by combining several ideas together.

THINK OUTSIDE THE BOX

If someone is stumped, they can try to tackle a problem from a different angle—this is known as lateral thinking. One example is to start with the most likely solution and try to work backward. Another is to ask why the problem occurred. For example, when the elk population in Yellowstone National Park exploded and began having a negative impact on the environment, scientists tried to reintroduce wolves, even though they were eradicated in the 1920s. This set off a domino effect of positive outcomes. It's a great example of what seemed a nonsensical idea proving to be a really smart thing to do.

GETTING CREATIVE

Creativity is the ability to come up with sparkling new ideas. Some may be trivial, others useful or life-changing. It's not just musicians, artists, and writers who are creative—many breakthroughs in science and math have come from creative thinking.

CREATIVE CONNECTIONS

No one part of the brain is responsible for brilliant bursts of creativity. It's more about different parts of the brain suddenly making connections to come up with the unexpected and original. With teenage brains undergoing lots of change and rewiring, it's no surprise that teens are among the most creative of all.

Hmmm...

...what should I write a story about today?...

Some people get a creativity boost by thinking in pictures or sketching out ideas that would otherwise be lists of words. This may prompt links and associations from memory not thought of before.

...I know! A purple pig's skateboarding adventures. Perfect!

...a flying fish? No, that's not silly enough...

COMING IN WAVES

The brain's electrical activity can be mapped by EEG machines. They use electrodes stuck to the scalp to produce wavy lines on a graph known as brainwaves. Beta waves are created when people are awake and normally busy. Gamma waves occur when people are at peak mental activity. Creativity most frequently happens when alpha waves are produced—usually at times when the brain is relaxed and the mind more open to new possibilities.

RELAX...

Famous composer Igor Stravinsky stood on his head to clear his mind before thinking up new music. Others prefer a brisk walk, bath, or simple cleaning or gardening chores to produce alpha waves. Taking a shower led NASA engineer James H. Crocker to come up with a way of fixing the Hubble Space Telescope in 1990 so that it took sharp photos instead of fuzzy ones.

BRAIN LAB

USE YOUR IMAGINATION

Flex your creativity by performing imaginative tasks. Why not alter the lyrics to a song, write the oddest story you can think up, or imagine what never-seen-before invention would most help the world. Try out "what if?" scenarios such as "What if pets could talk?" The brain spends a lot of time following the familiar. These sorts of thought experiments help get it out of a rut and set it free to think of original alternatives.

What if there was no gravity?

IT'S BEEN EMOTIONAL

Emotions are powerful sensations felt in the body. They are created by signals generated deep inside the brain. There are thought to be six basic emotions: fear, anger, surprise, disgust, joy, and sadness.

SURVIVAL TOOLKIT

The basic emotions occur without us consciously thinking about them. They evolved as ways to help early people survive. For instance, surprise may cause someone to focus all their attention on an object or situation, so they can judge whether it could harm or help them. Fear may give someone the energy boost to fight a threat, while disgust might force someone to turn away from rotten food that could be harmful.

| ANGER | HAPPINESS | SURPRISE | DISGUST | SADNESS | FEAR |

GETTING EMOTIONAL

Emotions are triggered by the brain's limbic system, which sends chemicals through the body to create physical responses. For example, the face may turn red when someone is angry or the stomach may churn and a person could feel sick when they experience disgust. These body reactions often come with facial expressions that other people can recognize.

MOODY MOMENTS

Powerful emotions usually don't last long. They prime the body for a quick reaction and then ease off. Milder but longer-lasting sets of feelings are called moods. The biased brain finds it easier to recall memories that match someone's mood—a reason why people may recall other bad memories when in a bad mood.

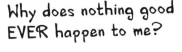

Why does nothing good EVER happen to me?

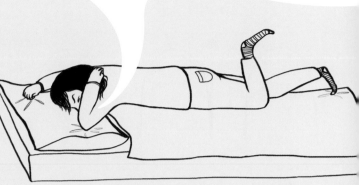

Er, it's great, just what I wanted.

EMOTIONAL ROLLERCOASTER

Most of the time, emotions come and go. Someone might be sad for a little while, then something will happen to brighten their mood. Other times, though, emotions might stick around for longer than we like, or they might start to feel overwhelming. If this happens, it's important for you to find someone you trust to talk about what's going on. That person might be a trustworthy grown-up, or the school counselor. People are there to help when it all feels like too much.

EXCITEMENT   EMBARRASSMENT   GUILT   PRIDE   SATISFACTION   JEALOUSY

IT'S ALL SO COMPLEX

People feel many other "complex" emotions, including pride, excitement, and jealousy. Some, like embarrassment and guilt, are often felt after a person has said or done something. These emotions can influence how people feel about a choice or action, which can allow them to learn from mistakes, or can make people feel ashamed about expressing themselves, when we should be proud to be us!

GETTING IT RIGHT

Being a teen is an emotional time. With more independence, teens encounter lots of new people, experiences, issues, and choices, meaning they'll have a whole bunch of decisions to make.

STUDY
SLEEP
Wrong
Right
YES!
NO!
Maybe
Definitely
LEFT
RIGHT
Make up
Break up

WHY AM I *SO* EMOTIONAL?

Teens go through many challenges and changes to their bodies, lives, opinions, and social groups, all of which can prompt strong emotions. At the same time, different parts of their brain are developing at different rates.

EMOTIONAL BALANCE

The emotion-generating limbic system forms early, but the prefrontal cortex (part of the frontal lobe), which helps control emotions, isn't fully formed until people reach their twenties. This brain region also helps people plan for the future and weigh and judge decisions. It means teens have all the emotions, but may not yet feel confident and comfortable expressing them.

NOW, NOW, NOW!

Emotions can cause teens to make sudden decisions without thinking about the future. They're not alone—people of all ages often make hasty decisions, preferring an instant reward to a bigger and better reward later. This is known as delay discounting.

But I want them NOW!

50% OFF
Starts Next Week

EMOTIONS AND MEMORY

Emotions influence the memories people recall to help make a decision. Memories with strong emotions attached are often better remembered and so seem more important. This can mean people don't pay attention to a less emotional memory—one which might contain useful information that is crucial to the decision.

OLDER PEOPLE RECALL MEMORIES OF THEIR EMOTIONAL TEENAGE YEARS MORE KEENLY THAN OTHER TIMES IN THEIR LIFE— THIS IS CALLED THE REMINISCENCE BUMP.

BRAIN LAB

EMOTIONAL TOOLBOX

When you're experiencing a strong emotion, it can be really tricky to think about anything else—but that can sometimes lead you to make decisions you probably shouldn't. Here are a few tips that might help next time you're feeling overwhelmed:

- Quickly identify the extreme emotion you were feeling.

- Think through what solution or outcome you wanted from the situation.

- Remove yourself from what's causing the emotion—such as walking away from an argument or something that upsets you.

- Take a time-out to slow your breathing and count to 10.

- Talk about what you felt with someone you trust.

PLEASURE AND RISK

The brain is one big pleasure seeker! It rewards us for actions that it feels help us develop and prosper (such as eating or surviving a risky situation) with a little buzz of pleasure.

REWARD CENTER

Deep inside the brain are parts that handle pleasure and rewards, including the nucleus accumbens and the ventral tegmental area (VTA). Collections of connected neurons, known as pathways, carry reward signals from these areas into both the frontal lobe of the brain, where we do lots of our thinking, and also to the hippocampus, which helps form memories.

PLEASURE CHEMICALS

Neurons in these pathways release neurotransmitter chemicals such as dopamine, serotonin, and endorphins, which give people senses of pleasure, happiness, or relaxation. These are rewards for certain behaviors and can prompt people into repeating the action later to gain another dose.

BIG THRILLS

The desire for thrills often reaches a peak in a person's teens because teen brains produce more thrill-seeking dopamine and are also more sensitive to it. This drives many teens into taking more risks and seeking out new rewards.

HIPPOCAMPUS

NUCLEUS ACCUMBENS

DOPAMINE PATHWAYS

VTA

Some people enjoy taking big risks and feeling fear from scary movies, extreme sports, and theme park rides.

RISKY BUSINESS

Taking some risks is perfectly natural behavior and can prompt people to ask questions, try new things with the possibility of failure, and experience new activities or people. Teens are wired to experiment and take risks as part of growing up and gaining independence. Judging which risks to take and how big a risk really is can be tricky, especially for teenage brains. They lack both the experience of older people's brains and also fully developed frontal lobes, which can act as "brakes" on risky behavior.

FITTING IN

Some teens aren't big risk takers but can suddenly do something that terrifies them or is dangerous. Why? Well, it often boils down to trying to impress others or fit in with a social group. Teen brains can be focused on how others see them and often rank the risk of being ignored or kept out of a social group higher than other threats to their well-being.

THIS WAY

FEAR, STRESS, AND PHOBIAS

Fear is one of the core emotions and a natural response everyone has. It's designed to keep us safe, but stress, fears and phobias can have a negative impact on the brain.

FEARSOME STUFF

A fear-filled brain can cloud a person's judgments. This may cause someone to greatly overestimate the risk something poses to them, just because they find it terrifying. More people, for example, are injured or killed by lawnmower or vending machine accidents than by sharks. Yet, because sharks frighten people, people overestimate their risk and may underestimate a far higher risk of something that doesn't seem scary, such as stray dogs.

PHOBIAS

A phobia is more than a simple fear. It's an overwhelming dread of something that makes a person want to do anything to avoid it, even though the real risk posed may be tiny. Some phobias are relatively common, such as the fear of spiders (arachnophobia), enclosed spaces (claustrophobia), or heights (acrophobia). Others are rarer, such as cheese (turophobia), clowns (coulrophobia), or buttons (koumpounophobia).

STRESSED OUT

Stress is the body's response to pressure or changes in a person's life. It might be caused by school, friendship, or work worries, or frustrations with ourselves or our family. Stress and emotions such as fear and anger can trigger the flight-or-fight response (see pages 68–69). Everyone suffers from stress at times. Sometimes it can motivate people to work harder or overcome a problem they've been putting off. But for some people, stress can be frequent, upsetting, and exhausting. It might stop them from sleeping, eating properly, or being their usual social selves. An extreme response to stress can be a sudden, intense surge of anxiety known as a panic attack. If you feel stress getting on top of you, it is time to seek help from someone you trust, or a professional.

FEEL "BETTER"

BREATHE – Find ways to relax, such as simple breathing exercises, to stop stress from escalating.

EXERCISE – Many people feel calmer and better after a good walk, run, or sports game.

TALK – Admit you're stressed and talk it over with others you trust.

TAKE ACTION – Be realistic, break down problems into small pieces, and tackle those you can.

ENJOY – Do something you really enjoy and get a time out from the stressful situation.

REST – Good-quality sleep can help put the causes of stress into perspective.

PHEW! That's BETTER!

67

FIGHT OR FLIGHT!

The body and brain are equipped with a giant red, flashing panic button. When triggered by a threatening situation, it can send the brain into overdrive. This automatic set of reactions is called the fight-or-flight response.

BRAIN
The brain is switched on and its alertness is at its maximum for someone to make split-second decisions. Sometimes, people will feel their temper rising.

EARS
The sense of hearing sharpens to listen out for any signs of danger.

The response begins in the tiny almond-shaped part of the brain called the amygdala. This commands the frontal lobe to analyze the threat while signals urge the adrenal glands to release a cocktail of chemicals (mostly hormones) to race around the body. These alter how the body works, preparing it for a sudden burst of effort to survive the sudden challenge ahead.

EYES
The pupils of the eyes dilate to let in more light so the person can get a better view of the situation. The peripheral vision (the edges of the eyesight) sharpens at the same time.

LUNGS
The breathing becomes faster but shallower, helping to get lots of oxygen into the blood.

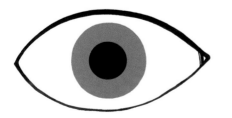

ONCE THE DANGER HAS PASSED, THE BODY

68

SURVIVAL!

Our ancient ancestors faced many physical, life-threatening dangers they had to fight or flee from, so it was a vital survival tool. However, it also kicks in when we face an emotional or mental threat, such as an exam, public speaking, or during a heated argument. Remember, this period of super stress will pass. Try to keep cool, think clearly, and not act rashly. See page 67 for some other handy stress-busting tips.

FACE
The skin may turn pale, as blood is diverted from just below the surface to the brain and muscles.

MOUTH
Dry mouth? That's right. The flow of saliva to the mouth decreases, as the digestive system partly shuts down. The brain has decided there are more important matters to deal with.

SKIN
A person may get sweaty yet their hands may feel cold and clammy. At the same time, their skin hairs may stand on end, giving them goosebumps.

ARMS
The major arm, shoulder, and leg muscles tense up ready to leap into action to help a person fight, tackle danger, or run away.

HEART
The heart starts beating faster, pumping oxygen and energy around the body more quickly.

CAN TAKE 15–60 MINUTES TO RELAX.

OUR WORLD

The human brain is so powerful it entirely shapes the world we perceive around us and how we interact with it. Since every brain is different, this means there are lots of ways to live in the world, and this includes some less common ways of being.

Who are you?

CAPGRAS SYNDROME SUFFERERS INSIST THAT THEIR LOVED ONES HAVE BEEN REPLACED BY IMPOSTERS.

STILL LIFE

For many people, vision is the dominant sense, but for some people, it works differently. People with akinetopsia, for instance, cannot see movement. Instead, they view the world as a long series of single, still images.

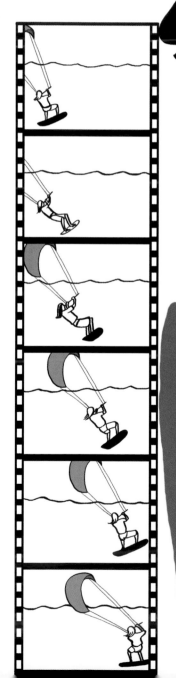

HALF THE WORLD

Some people with damage to one half of their brain interact with half the world around them. This hemi-spatial neglect means they cannot pay attention to signals sent from their senses on one side of their body. People with this condition may only eat one half of their plate of food, for example, or not notice objects to one side even though both of their eyes are functional.

FACE BLINDNESS

People with prosopagnosia cannot recognize and identify human faces or tell people apart—sometimes including themselves when they look in the mirror. Instead, they identify people by their voice or using their sense of smell, or using contextual clues like what they're wearing.

FUNCTIONAL PLASTICITY

Functional plasticity is when the brain alters connections between neurons to move functions from a damaged brain area to other areas. Some patients, for example, have regained the power of speech or arm movement after injury to the brain part that would normally handle them. The brain is super adaptable!

FEEL WHAT OTHERS FEEL

Mirror-touch synesthesia is when a person seems to experience the same sensations that another person feels. So if they see a person fall over, they will feel genuine pain, or if watching people hugging, they will feel hugged themselves. People with severe forms of this cannot bear watching others eating, as they feel their own mouths being crammed full of food.

ALIEN HAND SYNDROME

This condition sees a person lose control of one hand and arm, which seems to act on its own. People with this condition have been watched building something with their one controllable hand, only for the other hand to break it down.

BRAIN LAB

NO LONGER FAMILIAR

Most people's brains can sometimes make the familiar feel unfamiliar. Say a common word such as sheep, door, or coffee 40 times quickly. By the end, the word will feel and sound strange, almost as if you're encountering it for the first time.

CONCLUSION

We've come a long way since the ancient Egyptians pulled brains out through dead people's nostrils then threw them away with the other trash. Scientists have since learned that the brain controls all parts of the human body, forms and stores memories, manages thoughts and feelings, and makes all our decisions. Cool!

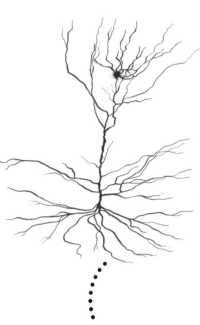

Could these
ROSEHIP NEURONS
be partly responsible for humans' great intelligence? Scientists will be hard at work studying them in the years ahead.

JUST THE START

There's still much more to learn, though, about how brains work and the huge diversity of brain function humans have. New breakthroughs are being made all the time, such as the 2018 discovery of a new type of brain cell only found in humans so far—the rosehip neuron.

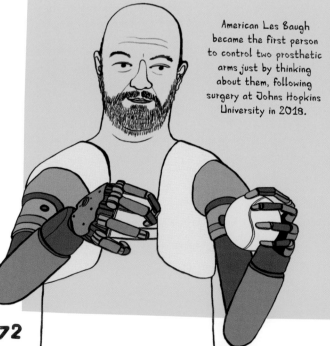

American Les Baugh became the first person to control two prosthetic arms just by thinking about them, following surgery at Johns Hopkins University in 2018.

THE MIND MACHINE

Future advances may involve new technology. Scientists are learning to connect brains to computers and other machines through links called neural implants. These channel electrical signals from nerves into electrical circuits to control the machine. Such implants have already enabled paralyzed patients to send emails just by thinking. Future implants might be able to bypass damaged areas of nerves, or even the brain, to enhance brainpower, for example, giving your memory a boost.

AuTHOR'S NOTE

So, there you have it: the incredible, extraordinary, and unique box of tricks in your head—your amazing brain. Cherish it, enjoy it, nurture it—and celebrate the true diversity of brains out there!

And speaking of you, I hope you have enjoyed reading this book as much as I did researching and writing it. I was so impressed with the human brain, with how it keeps on learning and improving, and the sheer volume of work it gets through each day. It's certainly made me think about how to get the most out of my brain in the future. After all, when you own nature's most complex and astonishing object, it would be foolish not to try, wouldn't it?

Has anyone seen my brain?

...it's packed full of neurOFFs rather than neurONs!

BRAIN GAMES

Consider yourself a budding brainiac or genius? Then try out these puzzles and questions designed to test different parts of your brain. Give yourself just 30 minutes to answer them all before turning to page 77 for the answers. No peeking or cheating!

1. Complete the missing numbers or letters in the following sequences:

a) A C E G I __ M
b) 1 2 3 5 8 __ 21 34

2. Answer these riddles:

a) I'm something that is broken when you call for me. What am I?
b) I belong to you, but others use me more often. What am I?
c) I have a mouth but cannot eat and a bank that doesn't hold money. What am I?

3. How can you move just three coins to make the triangle point upside-down?

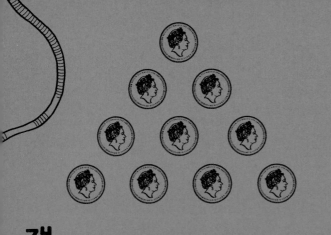

4. Unscramble these letters to spell out two parts of the brain:

a) puma chip sop   _____

b) metal blooper   _____ _____

5. How many cubes make up this figure?

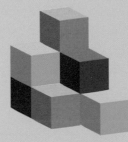

6. What's the name of the part of the brain highlighted in color?

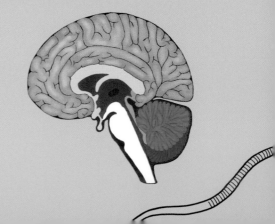

7. Looking at the pictures, can you figure out the weight on the fourth set of scales?

8. Can you figure out the number that should go in the final triangle?

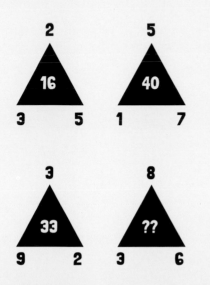

9. Without looking at the previous page, can you remember what the first word on that page is?

10. What number parking space is the car parked in?

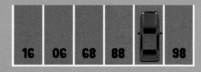

| 16 | 06 | 68 | 88 | | 98 |

11. Add two letters in the spaces to create two new words.

a) RIPE _ _ RIDE

b) LOUD _ _ ODES

12. Two parents have six sons and each son has one sister. How many people are in the family?

13. Can you figure out these common phrases or sayings from these word images?

a) MILLIO**1**N

b) C O U N T R y
   c O U N T R y

14. Can you join all nine dots using just four straight lines and without lifting your pencil from the page?

• • •

• • •

• • •

15. A person throws a ball as hard as they can. It comes back to them but hasn't bounced off anything. How is that possible?

IND OUT MORE

BOOKS

The Human Brain In 30 Seconds—
Clive Gifford, Ivy Kids, 2016

The Brain Book—Rita Carter et al, DK, 2019

Positively Teenage—Nicola Morgan,
Franklin Watts, 2018

Brain Games—National Geographic Kids, 2015

Body Works: Brilliant Brains –
Anna Claybourne, QED Publishing, 2014

FOR OLDER TEENS

**Inventing Ourselves: The Secret Life of the
Teenage Brain—**Sarah-Jayne Blakemore,
Doubleday, 2018

How Your Brain Works—New Scientist Instant
Expert, John Murray Learning, 2017

The Happy Brain—Dean Burnett,
Guardian Faber, 2018

WEBSITES

www.brainfacts.org
A website packed with news of new brain
discoveries and research.

www.dana.org/publications/factsheets
A fascinating collection of fact sheets on
different aspects of the brain and senses.

**www.healthychildren.org/English/ages-stages/
teen/Pages/Whats-Going-On-in-the-Teenage-
Brain.aspx**
Insights into the teenage brain on a
website that also gives advice on typical
teenage issues.

https://www.brainfacts.org/3d-brain#intro=true
Take a journey around an online 3D brain and
learn more about its parts.

www.bbc.co.uk/scotland/brainsmart/
Learn more about the brain along with some
useful tips for improving your memory.

VIDEOS

**www.ted.com/playlists/1/how_does_my_
brain_work**
A great collection of 14 TED talks on how the
brain works, including how you pay attention
and how the brain figures out where you are.

**www.pbs.org/wgbh/frontline/film/inside-the-
teenage-brain**
Watch a 50-minute Frontline documentary on
teenagers' brains.

www.youtube.com/watch?v=KkaXNvzE4pk
A five-minute animated feature on the
hippocampus and what happened to
the man who had his removed.

ONLINE EXPERIMENTS AND ACTIVITIES

**www.theverge.com/2017/12/4/16733778/
noisy-gif-hearing-movement-auditory-
neuroscience-synesthesia**

Appear to hear sounds when there are none with this animated synesthesia GIF.

www.youtube.com/watch?v=G-lN8vWm3m0

Watch this video of the amazing McGurk Effect—proof that what you think you hear can be shaped by what your brain assumes you see.

www.magicmgmt.com/gary/oi/index.html

Enjoy this great collection of interactive optical illusions.

**www.ncbi.nlm.nih.gov/pmc/articles/
PMC4255343**

A great collection of links to interesting brain websites.

All web addresses were correct at the time of printing. The publishers and author cannot be held responsible for the content of the websites, podcasts, and apps referred to in this book.

ANSWERS TO BRAIN GAMES

1. a) K,
b) 13

2. a) silence
b) your name
c) a river

3.

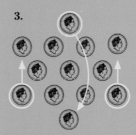

4. a) hippocampus
b) temporal lobe

5. 9

6. cerebellum

7. 27 lb (rabbit=3 lb, cat=7 lb and dog=17 lb)

8. 72 (the number in each triangle is produced by adding the bottom two numbers together and multiplying by the top number).

9. Brain

10. 87 (if you turn the page upside down, you'll see the parking spaces are numbered from 86 to 91)

11.
a) ST (RIPEST, STRIDE),
b) ER (LOUDER, ERODES)

12. Nine (Mom, Dad, six sons, and one daughter)

13. a) 1 in a million,
b) cross country

14.

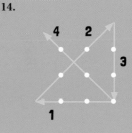

15. The person threw it straight up into the air

GLOSSARY

ADRENALINE
A hormone mostly made by the adrenal gland, which is released when the body is stressed or preparing a fight-or-flight response.

AMYGDALA
A small, almond-shaped part of the brain in the temporal lobe that is involved with emotions and memory.

ASSOCIATION
A feeling, memory, or thought connected with other thoughts or a person, place, or object.

ATTENTION
The ability to focus on one thing and filter out other things that might distract.

AXON
The part of a neuron (nerve cell) that carries a nerve signal away from the cell body.

BODY CLOCK
A sequence, run by hormones, which causes the body to behave in certain ways at particular times of the day.

BRAIN STEM
The lower part of the brain that connects the brain to the spinal cord.

CELL
One of the tiny units that living things are made up of. The human body consists of millions upon millions of cells of different types.

CEREBELLUM
The part of the brain that coordinates the body's movements and helps keep you balanced.

CEREBRUM
The largest part of the brain, responsible for handling thoughts, problem-solving, and the senses.

CORPUS CALLOSUM
A large bundle of nerves that connect the right and left halves of the brain.

DENDRITES
Finger-like parts of a nerve cell that carry a signal toward a nerve cell's body.

EEG
Short for electroencephalogram, this is a machine that measures the electrical activity of the brain using electrodes attached to a person's scalp.

EMOTIONS
Strong inner feelings and body reactions, including fear, surprise, and anger.

ENDOCRINE SYSTEM
A system of different glands that produce chemicals called hormones, which help control and maintain many parts of the body.

FILTERING
To sift through lots of thoughts and memories and to remove those that do not matter.

GLAND
An organ that produces a chemical for use in the body.

GLIA
Specialized cells in the brain and spinal cord which nourish and support neurons.

HORMONES
Chemicals produced by glands that carry messages to different parts of your body.

LIMBIC SYSTEM
A collection of different parts, deep inside the brain, which are involved in behavior, emotions, and memories.

MILLISECOND
One thousandth of a second

MOTIVATE
To cause someone to act or behave in a certain way.

NEURONS

Special cells that transmit nerve signals. Neurons make up much of the brain as well as your nervous system.

NEUROSCIENTIST

Scientists who study the brain and the nervous system and how they work.

PHOBIA

A constant, extreme fear of something that cannot be easily explained.

PREFRONTAL CORTEX

The outer layer of the front of your brain, which deals with planning and conscious thought.

PROPRIOCEPTION

The sense of knowing the position, location, and movement of the body and its parts.

REFLEX

An automatic action performed without thinking by a part of the body in response to something.

RETINA

Part of the back of the eye. It is packed with light-sensitive nerve cells that turn light into electrical signals.

SPATIAL AWARENESS

The ability to understand objects, distances, and space around you from all angles.

SPINAL CORD

A thick bundle of nerve fibers that run from the base of the brain through your spine.

SYNAPSE

A small gap between nerve cells across which signals can pass from one nerve cell to another.

THALAMUS

Part of the brain that relays signals from the senses to other parts of the brain.

THREE-DIMENSIONAL (3D)

To see things as having not just height and width but also depth.

VOLUNTARY

To do something that you want to do and are aware of, such as moving your hand to pick up something.

INDEX

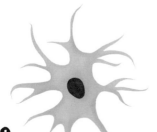